The Statue of Liberty:
51 Fascinating Facts
For Kids

Leanne Walters

This book is just one of a series of "Fascinating Facts For Kids" books. For more fascinating facts about people, history, animals and much more please visit:

www.fascinatingfactsforkids.com

Contents

The Idea

1. In April 1865, the American Civil War came to an end after four bloody years. The war had been fought over the issue of slavery and when peace came, slavery was abolished and America was united once more.

2. In France, Edouard de Laboulaye, a lawyer and expert in American history, was delighted that the war in America was over and that slavery had been made illegal.

Edouard de Laboulaye

3. Laboulaye was a great admirer of American freedom and democracy. He thought it would be a good idea if France gave America a monument

that celebrated liberty and the great friendship that existed between the two countries.

4. When Laboulaye held a dinner party at his home near Paris, one of the guests - a sculptor called Frédéric-Auguste Bartholdi - was so impressed by Laboulaye's idea that he volunteered to take on the task of designing and building a great statue.

Frédéric-Auguste Bartholdi

5. In the mid-19th century, the French people lived under a dictatorship and it would have been dangerous for a project celebrating freedom to have gone ahead. It wasn't until six years later that Laboulaye and Bartholdi felt it was safe enough to begin work on their statue.

Bartholdi in America

6.   In June 1871, Bartholdi set off for the United States to explain his idea to the American people. He met businessmen and politicians from all over the country who all seemed to be enthusiastic about the project.

7.   Bartholdi looked at many potential locations for the statue before deciding on a small island in the harbor of New York City - Bedloe's Island.

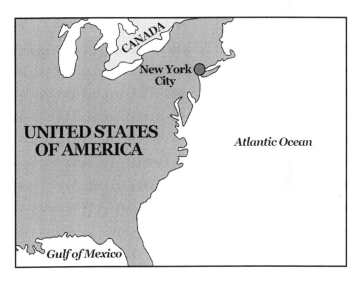

8.   Bedloe's Island was the perfect place for the statue. Standing in the middle of the harbor of America's biggest city, it would be seen by millions of people and would give a magnificent first impression of America to people entering the country by ship.

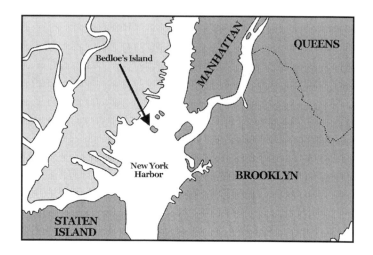

9. Bedloe's Island belonged to the government and Bartholdi would need permission to erect the statue there. After meeting the US president, Ulysses S. Grant, Bartholdi was assured that Congress would give permission for the project.

Ulysses S. Grant

10. After five months of traveling across America selling people his vision, Bartholdi returned to France full of enthusiasm and got to work on the design of his "Statue of Liberty."

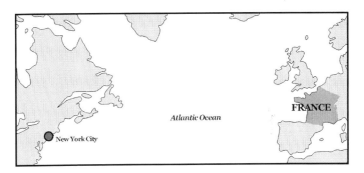

Bartholdi's Design

11. Back in France, Bartholdi told Laboulaye and other interested people about his time in America and what his plans were for the design of the statue.

12. Bartholdi proposed to build a gigantic statue more than 150 feet (45 m) high, and inside the structure there would be a staircase stretching all the way to the top. People would be able to climb its 354 steps and walk out on to a balcony where they could look out over New York Harbor.

13. Bartholdi designed his statue as a woman dressed in long flowing robes. It was based on images of the Roman goddess of freedom, Libertas.

The image of Libertas on an Ancient Roman coin

14. The statue's right arm would be raised high in the air holding a torch. The torch would symbolize the way to the future and also welcome people to the United States as they entered New York Harbor.

15. The left hand would hold a tablet which symbolized the important role of law in America. The tablet would have the date "July 4, 1776" inscribed on it - the date of the signing of the Declaration of Independence.

16. At the statue's feet would be a broken chain. The right foot would be raised to give the impression of walking toward freedom.

17. On the statue's head would be a crown surrounded by a halo of seven pointed rays - each ray representing one of the seven seas and the seven continents. The crown would have a platform which could give thirty people a magnificent view of New York Harbor and beyond.

18. Laboulaye and the others were delighted with Bartholdi's vision, and a committee was formed in order to raise money so that the construction of the statue could get under way.

Raising Money

19. One of the biggest problems with such an ambitious project was finding the money to be able to complete it. Bartholdi and the committee asked some of the wealthiest people in France for money, but after six months only a quarter of the funds needed had been raised.

20. Bartholdi traveled back to America where he was more successful than he had been in France. He convinced many people to help with the fund-raising and also got the permission needed from Congress to build the monument on Bedloe's Island.

21. When he returned to France, Bartholdi commissioned a gigantic painting of what the completed monument would look like when erected in New York. The people of France were so impressed that donations began to pour in. Bartholdi finally had enough money in place to begin construction of the statue.

Construction Begins

22. Bartholdi needed someone to design and build the inside of the monument and he engaged his former teacher - the architect Eugène Viollet-le-Duc.

23. Most statues and monuments were made from marble, stone, or bronze, but Viollet-le-Duc decided to use copper plates. Copper was both lighter and cheaper than other materials.

24. Unfortunately, Viollet-le Duc died soon after work began and Bartholdi turned to Gustave Eiffel, the brilliant architect and engineer who was to become well-known for his world-famous Eiffel Tower in Paris.

Gustave Eiffel

25.   Eiffel liked the idea of using copper for the skin of the statue, but made changes to the Viollet-le-Duc's original plans. He built a strong steel frame to which the copper plates were attached, and used sheets of asbestos to give protection from the heat of the Sun.

26.   The finished statue would be so large that it would be difficult to transport it the 3,600 miles (5,800 km) across the Atlantic Ocean to America. To get round this problem it was decided to build the statue in separate pieces that could be put together when they arrived in New York.

27.   In order to generate publicity for the project, Bartholdi and the committee decided that the finished pieces of the statue would go on show in both France and the United States, before being assembled in New York.

28.   The hand and torch were the first part of the statue to be finished, and in August 1876, they were shipped over to America to be exhibited at the World's Fair in Philadelphia.

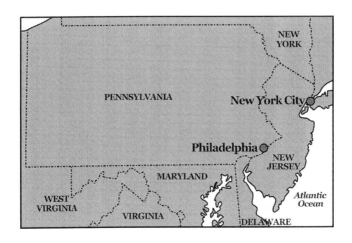

29. The hand and torch stood thirty feet (9 m) high and people paid fifty cents each to climb a ladder on the inside of the forearm. When they got to the top they could stand outside on the balcony that surrounded the torch.

The torch on display in Philadelphia

30. The Philadelphia fair ended in November 1876, and the hand and torch were taken to New York City. They were on show there for five years while the rest of the statue was being built back in France.

31. The head of the statue was finished in time to be exhibited at the Paris Universal Exposition of 1878. Visitors could climb to the top of the head and look out of the twenty-five windows that were built into the crown.

The head on display in Paris

32. The showcasing of the arm and head created a lot of interest in both France and America, and along with other fund-raising enterprises, enough money was made to complete the building of the statue.

The Pedestal

33. It had been agreed that America would be responsible for the building of a gigantic pedestal on which the statue would stand. A well-known architect named Richard Morris Hunt was chosen to design the base for the statue.

Richard Morris Hunt

34. Hunt designed a pedestal that would be eighty-nine feet (27 m) high and made of concrete and granite. More than 27,000 tons of concrete were used for the foundations and walls of the pedestal, and at the time it was the largest amount of concrete ever poured.

35. By June 1884, the construction of the statue had been completed back in France, but by the following March work on the pedestal had been halted. The project had run out of money and the government refused to give the $100,000 needed to finish the job.

36. Joseph Pulitzer, the owner of "The New York World" newspaper, decided to help get the pedestal completed and he donated $1,000 to a fund he set up to raise the money. He urged the readers of his newspaper to give money to the fund, however small the amount, and promised to publish the name of every donor.

37. People from all over America sent in what they could afford and by August 11, 1885, 121,000 of Pulitzer's readers had sent in the $100,000 needed to get the pedestal completed.

The Statue Arrives

38. While the pedestal was being built, the 350 separate pieces of the statue were being packed into 214 wooden crates to be sent by train to the docks at the port of Rouen. There, the crates were loaded onto "Isère," the French ship which would transport the statue to America.

39. On June 17, 1885, "Isère" arrived in New York Harbor carrying her precious cargo. Thousands of people cheered and waved flags as the ship docked at Bedloe's Island.

Isère arrives in New York Harbor

40. It took more than a year to finish the pedestal and assemble the statue, but on October 28, 1886, a great parade took place in New York City before the statue was officially opened to the public.

The pedestal under construction

41. The president of the United States, Grover Cleveland, made a speech at the unveiling ceremony and Frédéric-Auguste Bartholdi pulled on a rope to remove the French flag that was covering the statue's face.

The unveiling ceremony

42. Since that day in 1886, the Statue of Liberty has welcomed millions of people arriving in America by ship, and she has become a magnificent symbol of American freedom and liberty.

Assorted Statue of Liberty Facts

43. The statue's real name is "Liberty Enlightening the World" but it is commonly known as the "Statue of Liberty" or "Lady Liberty."

44. The statue was built to withstand all types of weather. She gets struck by lightning around 100 times a year and when a storm hits New York City she sways up to three inches side to side when winds reach fifty miles per hour (80 kph).

45. The statue's mouth is three feet (1 m) wide, each eye is two and a half feet (0.75 m) across, and each index finger is eight feet (2.5 m) long.

46. The seven continents represented by the rays on the statue's crown are - North America, South America, Europe, Asia, Africa, Antarctica, and Australia. The seven seas are all oceans - Indian, Arctic, Antarctic, North Atlantic, South Atlantic, North Pacific, and South Pacific.

47. It was originally planned to have the statue finished by 1876 in time for the 100th birthday of the United States, but it was not until ten years later that the statue was finally unveiled.

48. The friendship between France and the United States goes back to the American War of Independence of 1775-1783. The war was being fought against Great Britain, who ruled America at the time, and France sent money and supplies across the Atlantic Ocean in support. French soldiers even fought with the Americans against the British on the battlefield.

49. Twenty years after the death of Bartholdi in 1904, the Statue of Liberty became a national monument and in 1956 Bedloe's Island was renamed "Liberty Island," the name Bartholdi had always wanted.

The statue on Liberty Island

50. The Statue of Liberty could have been even taller. The original pedestal was designed to be 114 feet (35 m) high and made of solid granite. But it would have cost around $250,000 to build so a smaller, cheaper pedestal using concrete covered with a layer of granite was decided on.

51. When the statue was first built, it would have been a wonderful sight of gleaming copper. Unlike iron and steel, which rust over time, a blue-green coating called "patina" forms on the surface of copper. The exposure over many decades to weather, salty air, and sea water means that the statue is now a permanent blue-green color.

Illustration Attributions

Edouard de Laboulaye
Bibliothèque nationale de France [Public domain]
{{PD-1923}}

Frédéric-Auguste Bartholdi
Tucker Collection - New York Public Library Archives

Bedloe's Island (Fact 8)
Nafsadh [Public domain]

Ulysses S. Grant
Brady-Handy Photograph Collection, Library of
Congress [Public domain]

**The image of Libertas on an Ancient Roman
coin**
Classical Numismatic Group, Inc.
http://www.cngcoins.com
https://creativecommons.org/licenses/by-
sa/3.0/deed.en (changes made)

The Tablet (Fact 15)
Robert Scott Adams [CC BY-SA 4.0
(https://creativecommons.org/licenses/by-sa/4.0)]
(changes made)

Gustave Eiffel
USMC Archives from Quantico, USA [CC BY 2.0
(https://creativecommons.org/licenses/by/2.0)]
(changes made)

The torch on display in Philadelphia
Library Company of Philadelphia [No restrictions]

Made in United States
Orlando, FL
05 March 2023

30716754R00017